Painting Lilian

Painting Lilian

Copyright © 2016 Liane Chu Limited
All rights reserved.

ISBN: 0692445897
ISBN 13: 9780692445891
Library of Congress Control Number: 2016903306
Liane Chu Limited, Hong Kong

Commentaries:

"Train up a child in the way they should go and when they are old they will not depart from it." Proverbs 22:6. This book is a perfect reflection of this wisdom; parents who discerned their child's natural "bent" or inclination, and provided the guidance to develop and round out what has become a valuable life-skill. A delightful read full of wonderful cultural insights."

---**Sandra K. Scruggs**, Missions Pastor, Zion Dominion Global Ministries, Buffalo City, New York. CSR, New York State Supreme Court Reporter.

"Lovely stories that will inspire and guide any mother or mother to be, showing how the power of love and faith can influence a child's development."

---**Jessica Jordan**, Consul General of Bolivia.

"This is a story of love, faith and hope, which are the most precious things in our lives. This is a story of growing pains, which everybody is to experience."

---**Sheng Lu**, Executive Vice President at Shanghai Education Television Station, China.

"Inspiring story of a teenager coming of age, living in culturally diverse areas, all while dealing with a condition that presents with great social challenges."

---**Jian Jenny Tang M.D**. ASSISTANT PROFESSOR, Obstetric, Gynecology and Reproductive Science, Icahn School of Medicine at Mount Sinai Hospital, New York.

> "An authentic and heart-warming story that speaks of a teenager's true heart and how she overcomes challenges by remaining true to herself, having the courage to ask for help and choosing to be happy. It is every mother's dream for her child."

---**Anne von Behr**, Client Service Director at TNS Singapore, mother to two sons and a daughter.

> "I am reminded of the challenge and the learnings, the joy and the love in raising teenage daughters and how it has shaped the relationship we will have for our lifetime."

---**Steve DeRose**, Chair, Centre for Global Leadership, Villanova School of Business, Pennsylvania. Retired as VP Global Customer Development Excellence Unilever in 2012.

> "What a beautiful illustration of a mother and daughter's journey to overcome some of life's difficulties and how the love of family was enhanced. Lilian displayed strength by utilizing her own coping strategies and acknowledged when her unique struggle was too much to handle alone. Powerful!"

---**Holly Breach**, former educator, mother of three and friend.

> "An honest and pure insight into the life of a teenager. The book not only follows the struggles of Lilian's teenage years, but perfectly captures the extent to which the family and friends have impacted her life."

---**Ram Jayaveerapandian**, 2016 Student Council President, Dwight School New York.

"There is joy and sadness along the way of growing up. There is a smartness and wisdom of life in the story that everyone can relate to from the story of teenage girl, her music and her lyrics."

---**Leung Victor Chan**, VP and Laboratory Solutions Greater China General Manager, Agilent Technologies (China) Co. Ltd.

"For the first time in my life, I cried when I was reading a book. I am so touched by the story, how much love and faith that a family can share. If you are a mother or a teenage girl, you will definitely find yourself in Maggie or Lilian."

---**Jin En Malongna Chein**, VP of Learning and Innovation for Veolia China Ltd.

Table of Contents

Prologue · xi
Summary: Sketching Lilian · xiii

[Part I Love] · 1
Introduction: Love, Faith and Hope · 3
When truly loved, you can accomplish anything · · · · · · · · · · · · · · · · · 5
They were together and that was all that mattered· · · · · · · · · · · · · · · · 8
Life's a give and take · 11
My first painting lessons · 13
Family is everything· 14
Lunar New Year; About sticky cake and the color red · · · · · · · · · · · · 14
On the move again · 17
Tourette syndrome· 17
Humor and tap dancing to survive · 18
Having Tourette's taught me how to handle difficult situations · · · · · · 19
I became part of a solid group of friends· 21
A bird in a cage· 22
Making friends is about learning from them · · · · · · · · · · · · · · · · · · · 25
I don't have trust issues, I just know better · 26

[Part II Faith] · 31
Everything is going to be alright · 33
New York, concrete jungle where dreams are made of (Alicia Keys) · · · 33
Goodbye my darling Shanghai · 34
'I fell off my pink cloud with a thud' (Elizabeth Taylor) · · · · · · · · · · · 37
People in NYC were super friendly but I wasn't sure if they meant it · · 39
You have to peel off many layers to find the nice person underneath · · 39
Gossip Girl: We make our own fairytales · 40
My mom would call me lazy · 41

[Part III Hope] · 43
Surprise yourself with what you're capable of! · · · · · · · · · · · · · · · · · · 45
Eat your heart out · 45
What is bulimia precisely? · 46
They just didn't understand me · 49
Fighting my way up · 50
Only I could make myself happy again · 52
I sang her all the songs I had ever written · 53
I wanted to inspire young girls with my music · · · · · · · · · · · · · · · · · · 55
When we kissed, violins played · 58

Conclusion · 61
February 2016 - Living in the here and now · · · · · · · · · · · · · · · · · · · 61
Dear daughter · 67
About the Author · 71
Acknowledgement · 74

Prologue

*"Our deepest fear is not that we are inadequate. Our deepest fear is that we are powerful beyond measure. **It is our light, not our darkness that most frightens us.** We ask ourselves, 'Who am I to be brilliant, gorgeous, talented, fabulous?' Actually, who are you not to be? You are a child of God. Your playing small does not serve the world. There is nothing enlightened about shrinking so that other people won't feel insecure around you. **We are all meant to shine, as children do**. We were born to make manifest the glory of God that is within us. It's not just in some of us; it's in everyone. **And as we let our own light shine, we unconsciously give other people permission to do the same. As we are liberated from our own fear, our presence automatically liberates others.**"*

MARIANNE WILLIAMSON

The idea of this book came to life early 2015. Well, actually the idea of creating it had been lingering in the head of the initiator, Maggie Chan, even longer. Maggie has an amazing international career as a businesswoman and a senior leadership position at the multinational company - Unilever. She has a successful entrepreneurial husband with a multi-cultural background, and a lovable and talented daughter. At first sight, her life seems pretty perfect.

Maggie has always felt the need to give purpose to her life next to pursuing a business career. She was not born a princess herself and like a lot of career woman, she has fought her way up. Empowering women & being an inspiring working mother have always been important personal drivers. Combining it all is not always easy. Maggie experienced that especially when the family moved to New York City.

Maggie considers her daughter Lilian lucky to have lived in different key-cities in the world. Being exposed to a variety of countries and cities gives you a broader understanding of cultures and grows you as a person. But the impact of being confronted with cultural changes shouldn't be underestimated. New York is a vibrant and demanding city. It was a tough adjustment for the whole family, but especially for Lilian. She was 15 years old, a teenager, when she moved and although it was a wonderful experience, it has been extremely challenging as well.

This book takes you on a journey through a tough period in Lilian's life. Maggie and her husband have always provided Lilian with advice and guidance to make her resilient. But how do you guide your daughter through adversity? Maggie and Lilian went on a journey to rediscover Lilian; her passion, her talents and her ability to shine and enjoy 'being in the light' again.

Going through this period with her daughter has taught Maggie valuable life lessons. She felt the need to share it, as it might be beneficial to others. When Lilian agreed, she gathered a group of insightful people together to bring her story to life in this book.

Eva Lebens

Summary: Sketching Lilian

Lilian is a Chinese girl, born in Hong Kong. She is seventeen when she shares her story about love, faith and hope with us. Lilian is young, but has experienced more in her life than most people of her age. She might seem privileged, having parents with great jobs, living in an amazing apartment in New York city and attending a private school even Paris Hilton attended (okay, only for a while). But is she really? Lilian has the ability to reflect on her life and sees everything she goes through as a huge learning experience. She's honest and describes her life with a sense of humor you would only expect of adults. Lilian is an amazing artist, she's caring and girls of her age will definitely recognize themselves in her story. Moms will recognize their daughters in Lilian AND themselves in Lilian's mom, which makes it an interesting mother-daughter 'handbook'.

What does Lilian think about it? She summarized: 'Being fifteen is not easy. I can say that now being seventeen. Being seventeen is not easy either; you're not really a teenager anymore, but you're not quite an adult either. People don't seem to value your opinion (yet), even if it's better than that of any adult in the room. Being 'only' seventeen, people think you just started your life, that you are inexperienced. I can hear them think; 'Really, what does she know?!' I've heard it many times. It's just an opinion and I of course see the difference between my mom's colleagues, friends and me. On the other hand, I do believe I have a story to tell. It's NOT a unique story, because I'm just Lilian, I'm just a normal girl. But I have experienced some rough ups and downs that taught me a lot. My darkest periods in hindsight might have been the biggest learning experiences in my life. I wish my mom had had a book like this when I went through my dark period. It would have made both our lives so much easier!

[Part 1 Love]

Introduction: Love, Faith and Hope

Sometimes I feel overwhelmed by everything that happens around me. The world moves so rapidly and people are everywhere, running around like ants in search of food. Where do they go, what sparks them, what is their goal in life? It makes me a bit nervous as it introduces the question: Where do I go? What is my passion? What are my hopes in life, my loves, my fears? Whenever I feel overwhelmed I feel the need to create art. I often write music or paint at night during the dark hours when even NYC quiets down for a little bit. Those are my magical hours in which 'I wash away from the soul the dust of everyday life,' as Pablo Picasso said.

Creating art has a mysterious touch to it. When painting, I start with an empty sheet or an empty canvas and notice how my pencil flows over the paper almost uncontrollably. Whatever seems like total chaos in my head unfolds itself to paper as if it was meant to be. The feeling it gives me is comparable to falling in love; I literally feel butterflies in my stomach when the things in my head turn into magic. I first set up the painting in rough lines and then I fill in the bigger parts; dark, light, bold strokes, aggressively sometimes. Finishing a painting and completing the details is my favorite part. I sometimes turn on loud music and dance to celebrate a new work.

Creating art is my life and it's a reflection of life at the same time. Georgia O'Keeffe said: 'To create one's own world takes courage' and I do so agree. Although I think it goes for both creating art and living life. You never know in advance where you go, or where it ends. You just start, write the first sentence of a song or place a first stroke with your brush and off you go! I guess the essence is not to think too much about it. Enjoy, don't worry about the mistakes you will definitely make but embrace them. Have confidence that you will deal with mistakes and that they will only make you stronger.

It sounds fairly logical and yet I have been struggling to keep it together the past two years. Even my art couldn't come to the rescue at one point in time. I could write songs and I still painted, but those works definitely reflect the rather dark period I went through. I blamed my new school, I blamed loves and I blamed my parents. I basically blamed everything and everyone for my misery. Only when I stopped doing that and realized that only I can make myself happy, things changed. I started to focus, made decisions and communicated with my parents (especially my mom) again. I noticed that I started feeling okay, that I could love myself which was the key to opening up to others. Feeling loved finally gave me the power to bring my art projects to a different level.

This is my story about love, faith and hope.

When truly loved, you can accomplish anything

So this book is about me, Lilian Chu. I was born in Hong Kong in the year of the Ox, meaning I have to work hard to accomplish things in life. I like to call myself Liane. It sounds better because it's shorter and easier to pronounce. Secretly I like having an artist name and the fact that people have to put a little effort in tracing me down. My mother likes to call me 'bao bei' which is Chinese and literally means 'precious sea shell'. Most Chinese mothers use it in the meaning of 'precious baby'. It's sweet as long as she uses it at home and not when we're in a public setting. My Chinese name is Chu Lai Ching. Lai means beautiful, Ching means sunshine and my name also relates to my dad's name which I will explain later.

I love to practice art and judging by the opinion of respected others I'm reasonably good at it. I don't take myself too seriously and I live for my friends; they fuel my fire and I learn a lot from them. I'm also the daughter of hard working Chinese parents (read a bit more about them and our Chinese names in the frame) who mean the world to me, but also raised the bar for me. They studied hard and work even harder, and they expect me to do the same, they won't easily give me a break. I'm also Lilian who suffers from Tourette's syndrome, fought bulimia nervosa and moved around the globe in the meantime. Oh and I'm a bit skeptical about love. Does true love still exist nowadays I often wonder. Even though my mom and dad's love-story is the best in the world:

My parents met for the first time in December 1992. My dad arrived at the train station of the Chinese University of Hong Kong. He had just moved to Hong Kong and asked this young lady, my mom, the way to the registration office. My mom claims he asked the girl standing next to her first. My dad says that might be possible, but with one goal in mind: to get in touch with my mom. He instantly adored her and to put it in his words: 'A true player doesn't play.' To him it was love at first sight. My mom showed him the way to the registration office. Or actually, she showed him the wrong way at first as she was nervous, which to me is an indication that she must have instantly felt something for him too. They exchanged beeper numbers (can you believe it, a beeper!) And when he beeped her later that evening to thank her, she invited him to join her and her friends for tea. He did and that's how their relationship started. My mom admired my dad, and they went almost everywhere together; my dad even took her to Italy before they were married, which definitely was progressive for that time. It drove her parents crazy in the beginning, as they were protective of their daughter; was she safe with him? Of course she was. They were just young and very much in love. They still are.

The Chinese University of Hong Kong train station, this is where my parents met.*

My mom's name is Chan Ping Maggie. Maggie is her Christian name. 'Ping' means she has a soothing purity like jade and that she is 'crystal clear' as in 'ice'. Her parents wished for her to be a person who is true to herself and others and relatable. My mom is humble, generous and open-minded. She is somewhat quieter than my dad, although I've seen her with her friends a few times lately and she can be quite loud as well! My mom was born in Xiamen (China) in the year of the pig. If you look it up you will find that pigs can easily be fooled. Being born in the year of the pig also means that she won't easily give up. If she sets a goal she will follow through no matter what; she is persistent and reliable. My mom is a super woman and my best friend. I share 98% of my life with her. I need that 2% for me, although I couldn't tell you what I don't share with her. She guides me through difficult times in my life.

My dad is Chu Hsiung Shih Yuan. Yuan (Shih Yuan in Chinese) is his Christian name and means 'far away'. Shih means 'world'. His parents wished for him to have big dreams and discover the world. My dad's second name is Yun Kai. My mom and I don't have a second name. A second name was given in the old days and often traced back in the family history. Yun Kai means 'open cloud' like opening up the sky. My parents wished my name to relate to my dad's name and gave me the name Lai Ching; the beautiful sunshine you see and feel when the clouds part. My dad was born in Taiwan and a descendant of the Aixinjueluo clan, the imperial clan of the last emperor of the Qing dynasty. To me, he's definitely born for adventure. He was a Karate champion when he was only 17 and still loves to be active. He's a great dancer and organizes salsa dance conferences in Asia, South America and recently in New York. A salsa dance conference consists of salsa performances and workshops. He is a 'cult of personality', people admire him, they simply want to follow him because he's that inspirational. He was born in the year of the goat, which means that he is hard working, smart and intelligent. My dad lights my fire and ignites my dreams.

My great grandmother,
Wei Xuan Aixinjueluo
愛新覺羅蔚宣

At my grandparents' home,
North Point, Hong Kong

They were together and that was all that mattered

It is actually quite amazing my parents met at all as they have very different backgrounds. My mom grew up in Hong Kong and my dad is Chinese, born in Taiwan, but as explained above, South America is rooted in him as well.

My mother was born during the Cultural Revolution in China. The political situation was not very stable at that time. People - especially free thinkers, such as intellectuals and artists - had to be cautious to voice their opinion. Communism was restored and had to replace the rise of what was called 'capitalism'. A lot of people went to Hong Kong in search for freedom and a better life. Lots of them never returned to China because Hong Kong became their home. The same happened to my mother's parents. In 1979 my grandmother left for Hong Kong with my mother and her elder brother carrying an equivalent of only five dollars in Chinese Renminbi (RMB) with them. They moved in with my great grandparents after leaving mainland China. They were very lucky that my great grandparents already lived there! My grandfather joined them two years later. They lived in an 830 square feet three-bedroom apartment with four families - all relatives - of which six children. Altogether 14 people shared that little space. Being together was all that mattered.

North Point, Hong Kong*

Not speaking Cantonese (the native language in Hong Kong) or English, they had a difficult time integrating. It only encouraged my mom to work harder in school. At the age of eight she already knew she could save on tuition fees if she would be the best student of her year. She attended prestigious schools, and went to study at the Chinese University where she eventually met my dad.

My dad is an entrepreneur and polyglot. He speaks English, Spanish, Mandarin, Portuguese, Cantonese and Italian fluently. He was born in

1967 in Taipei - Taiwan and has two younger brothers. His father, my grandfather, was a poet & a pilot. When my father was nine, the family decided to follow my grandfather's dream to be closer to nature and moved to Trinidad-Beni in Bolivia. They started a few businesses including a Chinese restaurant, but the most interesting business definitely was founding the world's smallest commercial airline of which my grandfather was both the pilot and the flight attendant! It was in Bolivia that my dad developed a love for Latin music and salsa dancing.

Bolivia became economically in tumultuous and politically unstable over the years, which forced them to leave the country. They moved to Europe (Italy and Portugal) in 1986. The family got into the marble and granite business and exported to the booming Chinese market of the 1980's. My grandfather supported my dad to study in the USA and after graduating he started working for the family owned marble and granite company. It turned out to be a wise decision that greatly impacted his life. The business brought him to Hong Kong to study Chinese and that - indeed - is how he met my mom.

So, yes, my dad is adventurous and you can definitely say that both my mom and dad like to be busy. It's something that I inherited from them, although I like to be lazy and love sleeping as well!

Painting Lilian

One of the salsa events organized by my father in
Shanghai 2015 – www.Salsamemucho.com

Life's a give and take

My parents' marriage is solid. They make jokes, especially my dad and of course my mom believes them all as she's very gullible, something which I definitely inherited from her. My mom always tells me that you have to be willing to accept and compromise when it comes to sharing your life with someone else. It's a give and take and you will sometimes have to sacrifice, but in a healthy relationship you will get valuable things in return as well. She believes that people are different and that there are things you can't change and thus have to accept. My dad has his own version. He will tell you that he's the head, but that he could never function without my mom because she's his neck. It must be a man's way of expressing love, I definitely like my mom's version better.

This picture is my parent's wedding picture. It looks like my dad is super tall, but it's actually an illusion as my mom is sitting in a chair! They

11

always joke about it. Whenever someone says something about it, they will tell you how they met, again. Consider this a warning.

My parents, photo taken in March 1997, Hong Kong.

The first few years of their marriage they worked hard. They lived in a tiny apartment in a popular suburb of Hong Kong, Shatin. My dad was running a trading company in Iquique in Chile and my mom pursued her career as a trainee at a multinational company. They didn't see each other that often as my dad travelled a lot. During her pregnancy - that came sooner than expected - my mom only saw my dad once. She's always been very independent though and she spent time with her parents who helped her a lot.

My first painting lessons

I was born on December 12th, 1997. My mother wanted to start her three months maternity leave as late as possible in order to enjoy most of her 'free' time after giving birth. Her water broke on her last day of work though. My dad couldn't be there for the delivery as he was traveling back from Chile. He did arrive right after I was born and even saw me before my mom. My mom had a caesarian section and while the doctors were running some tests on me, my dad rushed in. My mom spent a month in bed at her parents' house. According to Chinese tradition the grandparents take care of the newborn for the first month during the day while the newborn mom has time to recover and ease into her new life with a baby. After three months maternity leave, my mom went back to work. My parents could pursue their careers as if nothing had happened because my grandparents and very sweet Indonesian nannies took care of me. Our nannies always lived with us. I even shared a room with my nannies until I was 12. This might sound strange, but it is perfectly normal in Hong Kong. The nanny took me to school, prepared my dinner and showed me around town. I especially loved our first nanny, Eckor, who would take me to wonderful tiny local Indonesian shops. It's those hidden gems that I still like best and you would never ever find on your own. Oh my gosh, it reminds me of *Soto Ayam*, that really is my forever favorite Indonesian dish. I did see my parents during the week, but they worked long hours. I mainly spent quality time with them in the evenings and on the weekends. It was a given and very much embedded in the modern Asian culture where both parents have a full-time job.

With Eckor in Hong Kong

My mom has always actively helped me in finding my passion. She had noticed that I was pretty good at figure drawing; and arranged for me to have painting lessons for a few hours on Saturday mornings from the age of two. The daughter of a famous Chinese painter happened to live in the same building as us and that's how I was first introduced to paint brushes, pencils and drawing techniques. My dad has always showed me that you have to put an effort in reaching your goal. He always supports me along the way and gives me inspirational books about bigger topics I'm struggling with. Giving me a book even became a yearly tradition. The book 'How to Make Friends' especially made a huge impression on me. My parents guide me in the decisions I make, even though I notice that I make quite a few decisions on my own nowadays.

Family is everything

My parents and grandparents had to fight their way up. They pushed themselves and never sat back. They did it out of love for their families. Their stories taught me to dream, believe in myself, be thankful and help others. And of course they showed me that family is everything. The family stays together and supports each other no matter what. Even if family members are not physically near to support you, knowing that you're loved means you can accomplish anything. I guess this is also why the Chinese New Year (Lunar New Year) plays a significant role in Chinese society. I've added some information about the meaning of this holiday that is comparable to Thanksgiving for Americans.

Lunar New Year; About sticky cake and the color red

Lunar New Year is the most important Chinese holiday celebrated at the turn of the Chinese calendar. People start preparing a month prior to the actual festivities. For me it starts with a buzz of excitement in the streets four or five days before the actual New Year's festivities. You can feel it in the air, the roads get busier and the crowds heavier until noise literally surrounds you everywhere. People are laughing, chatting and there's the constant popping sound of firecrackers.

Lunar New Year is also known as 'Spring Festival' because it's about welcoming spring and the beginning of the agricultural seeding season. The festival brings family and friends together; it feels like a reunion. Everyone goes out to visit loved ones to wish them well and share New Year's greetings. People wish each other prosperity amongst other good and positive things using a special idiom consisting of four word sentences. Red envelopes with money are passed out during the Chinese New Year's celebrations from married couples or the elderly to youngsters. It is also common for adults or young couples to give red envelopes to children. The red color symbolizes good luck and is supposed to ward off evil spirits.

Food plays a large part in the celebration of the festival and all regions have their own traditional food. The traditional cake 'Nian Gao' is made nationwide. It literally means: 'rise higher with each year'. Phonetically 'Nian' sounds like 'sticky'. According to the legend, the monster 'Nian' would come on the first day of New Year to devour livestock, crops, and even villagers, especially children. That's why people pop firecrackers to scare it away and put a very sticky cake in front of their door such that Nian's teeth would stick together after taking a bite. There's a sweet and a savory variant. The savory one is made of sticky rice flour, mushrooms, white radish and preserved pork that is comparable to salami. The sweet one is made with sticky rice flour and sugar cane.

Nian Gao年糕Lunar New Year Cake *

Everyone makes an effort to look good and we preferably wear new clothes. Literally everything is new, even the underwear. According to ancient Chinese superstition, you will have a challenging year coming up when your Zodiac year comes round. According to Chinese tradition you'd better make sure to wear something red as that is the color that will minimize the challenges that might come up. In 2009 (when I was 12) it was the year of the Ox, which is my Zodiac year and I definitely made sure to wear red things. It will be my Zodiac year again in 2021!

Weblog post. Moonlightened Way. N.p., n.d. Web*

You have probably seen or heard about the dancing lion climbing a ladder. It's a traditional feature too and especially important for businesses and start-ups. The lion symbolizes energy and his agility indicates that he can overcome challenges. Those are important aspects for businesses to grow!

Well, now you know a bit more about one of the main Chinese traditions, also my forever favorite holiday!

16

On the move again

My grandparents believed that their move to another country would eventually be beneficial. They believed that better education would provide a better life for their children. It was a struggle, but they always trusted their decisions and were brave out of love for their family. So did my parents when they thought the time had come to move to a quieter place within the busy city of Hong Kong.

I was five years old when we moved from downtown Hong Kong to Discovery Bay, a bay on Lantau Island. You have to take the ferry from Hong Kong Island to reach it. Lantau Island is less polluted and there's more space. My parents often visited Lantau Island before I was born and dreamed of raising a family there. When they got the chance to move there, they were over the moon! For me it was less exciting. I had a hard time making new friends and I missed my grandparents with whom I used to spend a lot of time. My parents kept telling me that I would be all right and I just had to be patient. And so I was. The school I attended put an effort in organizing art and drawing lessons and I remember successfully participating in a poster competition. I was so happy, I had never won anything in my life! At the same time I made some good friends whom I still visit whenever we go home over the holidays.

Tourette syndrome

On Lantau Island I also discovered something else. All of a sudden I started making strange noises. My mom says I sounded like a barking puppy! I remember my mom asking me what I was doing, but I had no clue what she was talking about. I didn't really notice it and couldn't stop either. Then it dawned on her: I had Gilles de la Tourette, just like my father. There had always been a high chance as it's a genetically transferred disease. My mom was shocked and upset. She's a problem solver and Tourette syndrome is not something you can solve; there is no cure, you just have to deal with it.

Most people know Tourette syndrome from the loud swearing, but there's more to it than that. Gilles de la Tourette is a neuropsychiatric disorder, which causes a person to make repeated, quick movements (such as blinking with the eyes) or sounds (like grunting or humming) that they cannot control. Those sounds or movements are called 'tics'; some people swear and some people shake their arm uncontrollably. I always describe it the same way my dad explains it to people:

'It's like having a mosquito bite. You can choose to scratch it, but you can also choose not to scratch it although it's very hard to resist the temptation. Eventually the urge to scratch will go away, but sometimes you 'have to' let the tic out.'

My mom was afraid of the effects of Tourette syndrome: Would people look at me differently? Would I be able to make friends? Could it get worse? She was ready to seek help from doctors. My dad, suffering from the syndrome himself, was very persistent we not visit a doctor. He had faith in a good outcome. Doctors would only give me medication, which he believed would only cure the symptoms and not the underlying problem. He convinced my mom that they would be able to guide me and figure out how to deal with it by themselves.

Humor and tap dancing to survive

The most important thing for me was to diminish the amount of food that aggravated the symptoms. I started a sugar free diet without the added artificial ingredients. Abiding by a Paleo diet - which means eating whole and unprocessed food - is probably the best you can do. It's not easy and can be a bit boring but it helps and I still try to stick to it. When I cheat and eat ice cream for example, or when I'm stressed or super excited, I will notice that the symptoms worsen. My dad also suggested I take tap-dance lessons to release my energy. I thought it was a pretty strange idea, but I loved it. Being physically active was relaxing and whenever I had a tic you wouldn't easily notice as tap-dancing allows room for strange movements.

My mom prepared me for possible responses in a fun way. We thought of different ways people might respond to my symptoms and created a role-play based on that behavior. It was her way of helping me (the problem solver, ha ha) and building my confidence. She believed that practicing how to deal with this would prevent me from being embarrassed. It really helped me and we both thought that ignoring peoples' stares and remarks would be the best way to deal with it. Practice overruled theory though as in real life I often made a joke about it. I had this tic that I shook my arm and I remember joking that I was so strong that I could open everyone's bags of chips. It became a running gag; all the kids gave their chips to me. I guess by making jokes, I took control over the situation. Recognizing my differences and believing it's actually no big deal having this disease, gave me power and faith in a good outcome.

Having Tourette's taught me how to handle difficult situations

What I also noticed and especially surprised my mom (as she told me recently) is that most people didn't really care, nobody made a big deal out of it! Of course there were exceptions and there's one incident I remember clearly. I was in first grade when the symptoms hit me during an exam. I started kicking my legs and I screamed as well. The teacher asked me what I was doing and why I did it. Of course I couldn't stop and afterwards I told my teacher about my disease. She didn't believe me even though the whole class supported me. She eventually went to the Dean, who also confirmed that it is caused by my disease. I guess for situations like this, the preparation I did with my mom helped a lot.

I believe no one will ever choose to suffer from a syndrome. I hope my symptoms will lessen when I get older, which statistically is likely to happen. On the other hand, I do believe it allows me to be more creative than 'normal' people because people with Tourette have a very active nervous system; our minds work faster and we think differently. I also learned from a young age that you always have a choice how to handle difficult situations. Making fun of myself became my survival too! It allows me to make others smile and it makes me happier at the same time. Making a difficult situation fun immediately changes 'not nice' into 'nice'. It gives me freedom because it makes me strong and independent. This is definitely something that would come in handy later, moving around the globe.

Discovery Bay Hong Kong*

Tap Dance Performance in Hong Kong 2005

I became part of a solid group of friends

I was ten years old when we moved again, this time to Shanghai. My parents decided to leave the idyllic Lantau Island and move to mainland China. It was the country my grandparents wouldn't think of living in again, but my parents had good reasons to move. My dad had already been doing business in China for a long time and my mom was offered a very good job relocation. They had faith that it would be a big step for all of us, being closer to our roots. I didn't want to go as I didn't understand why we had to leave home. I just loved my happy life under the guidance of my grandparents and being close to my friends.

Shanghai was a totally different city than any city we had lived in. Where Hong Kong has mainly new and high-rise towers, Shanghai has old, new, high-rise and low buildings all mixed together. It is also six times bigger than Hong Kong and the population is about three times higher, counting 20 million inhabitants. The roads are incredibly busy with cars, bikes and cyclists. The difference in buildings and the diversity in traffic make it extremely difficult to find your way. It's impossible to drive yourself as a foreigner. And we were certainly not considered 100% locals, coming from Hong Kong. You could compare the differences between Hong Kong and Shanghai to the cultural differences between European countries.

We moved into a three-story house in Hongqiao and we even had a front and back-yard. For the first time in my life, I had my own room because our new nanny had her own room as well. I was over the moon, it really was a princess room! The 'only' thing I had to do was make new friends; something I dreaded but eventually turned out to be a life changing experience.

Shanghai Homes : 2008-2012*

A bird in a cage

Because of the bigger space, my parents invited colleagues and friends over more often than in Hong Kong. Your home in general can play a big role in Shanghai. Being invited to someone's home means that you're treasured as a special friend by the host. The home is also considered a private and safe place and there just aren't a lot of places to go. I do remember this change, the house used to always be full. My parents always included me whenever they had friends or colleagues over during the weekend. Just as their parents used to do, they encouraged me to come out of my room and join the group. I remember sitting curled up on a sofa and listening to the stories the grown-ups shared. I am aware now that I learned so much from

Painting Lilian

those get-togethers. It has taught me that you need a social circle; it's fun, opens doors and meeting people from different backgrounds and different cultures helps you understand others better. I followed my parent's example and invited a lot of my friends to our Shanghai house.

Okay, I only followed their example after a while. In the beginning, maybe even the first year, I hid in my room where I played the guitar. I was 12 years old when I wrote my first song: 'Bird'. My mom would have loved for me to play the piano, but I just didn't like it, the guitar is so much more romantic and cool, and you can take it anywhere with you. By the way, my song about the bird is different from the story about our pet bird. Our bird in Shanghai is very cheeky: we thought we bought a male bird but turned out to be a female. And if this made you curious, read the whole story and song in the frame!

The party at Shanghai Home 2008 (Maddy is next to me on the right)

My bird Mambo (i.e. Mamboritta)

Bird

Download the "QR code" app, and scan this QR code to listen the song

I am sitting here and look outside the window, playing my guitar. I see a blue blue sky, oh a bunch of birds are flying around.

#They make me so dizzy, they make me SHA LA LA, they make me WA A A, they make me ooh ooh.

I want to be a bird, flying in the sky, I want to be a bird, flying in the sky, bird # So I am sitting here, running out of words, don't know what to sing. I see the sun up high, Oh a bunch of birds are flying around.

I was thrilled to get a pet. We had a choice of two parrots at the pet-shop; one was pretty and quiet and the other was wild and had quite a temper. My dad suggested to take the wild one, because he thought it would never be sold otherwise and he felt bad for it. We called him Mambo and he was chained to a large stand in my room. Mambo was a funny bird, he acted quite weird and whenever music played he would sing and wiggle to it. Sometimes we attempted to let him fly freely, but he didn't really fly, it seemed that he couldn't, or maybe he just didn't feel like it. One day he made a really funny noise, tweeted differently and all of a sudden he laid an egg! We were flabbergasted! We figured that he, or well, SHE, must have had a party with the other birds in the garden when we let Mambo out to get some fresh air and a sunbath, which is good for his feathers. From that day onwards we named Mambo, Mamboritta. Before we left Shanghai we made sure to find Mamboritta a good home and had her adopted by a salsa dance studio owned by a friend of my dad.

Making friends is about learning from them

After a while my mom advised me to organize a barbecue for all my friends from the compound and school. Even though I dislike being urged in a certain direction, this indicated the start of having wonderful friendships. I guess parents sometimes are right. My dad has always emphasized the importance of being open-minded in friendships. He has always encouraged me to befriend a wide variety of people; old and young, men and women, rich and poor and across cultures and nationalities. Making friends is about learning from them, about becoming a more inclusive person. Of course I also have a book about communicating and how to do that with people of various backgrounds on my shelf - that indeed, my dad gave to me.

The first person I really connected with was a teacher. Maybe he was more like a mentor to me than a friend but I definitely learned a lot from him. Mr. Sein was my art teacher in 8th and 9th Grade and stopped me using an eraser. I hated it! He was persistent and asked me if I could erase my mistakes in life? Well, no, of course I couldn't. I can still hear him say: 'Well, if you find ways to deal with the mistakes you make in life, then you should learn to do exactly that in your art pieces, Lilian.' Oh and the following: 'Everyone makes mistakes. The way people deal with them separates the brilliant from the average. The same goes for artists. A good artist can embrace every mistake and make it into something fabulous.'

It was a huge step forward creating art. After a year I noticed that I was so much faster than the other students. I still hardly use an eraser nowadays and Mr. Sein still is a source of inspiration to me, his artwork is amazing. Mr. Sein grew my confidence, which opened doors in making more friends.

I made many friends but only a few special ones. I'm the kind of person that rather has a few good friends than tons of semi-good ones. I prefer to be surrounded by inspiring, very talented, smart people - as they often teach me new things - the ones that go the extra mile for each other. There are some things in friendships that are non negotiable and will always be important. Trust maybe the most important one. My first crush made that painfully obvious.

I don't have trust issues, I just know better

I was thirteen and we had been living in Shanghai for a while. I started making friends at school and in the compound where we lived. One of my girlfriends in the compound suggested meeting her brother. We met and I could definitely sense that he liked me. He was funny and made me laugh so loud, which made me kind of fall in love with him. I think we shared a similar kind of humor; I like being silly and not taking things too seriously and he did too. My friends kept on saying that we looked so cute together and that we should be boyfriend and girlfriend, but I had no clue what that meant! One day we were going for a walk and my friends decided to hide in the bushes, because they were wanted to see what would happen. Would he kiss me? Right at that time I stepped in dog's poo and it didn't feel romantic at all! Then the boy took my hands and asked me to be his girlfriend! Seriously, I wouldn't have had a clue what to do if he had kissed me. I really liked him and from that moment we held each other's hands wherever we went and were a 'couple'! Or so I thought.

A few weeks later I ran into his friends while participating in a badminton tournament. I enthusiastically asked them about him and they said: 'Oh yeah, he's very nice, but he has a girlfriend'. I remember thinking, yes I know, duh, that's me! Then they said her name. I must have looked so puzzled because they didn't mention my name but the name of another girl!! Suddenly it dawned on me, he was cheating on me! I couldn't believe it. I confronted him and he didn't even try to lie about it. He admitted it, just like that. I cried a million tears, I was so sad. Writing a song (Forget You - see the Frame for the song) and exercising helped me to get it back together. This first crush and another I will get to later, are the main reasons why I'm a bit skeptical about love.

Forget you
Scan the QR code on page 24 to listen the song

Lying on the couch
Looking at the clouds
And hope you walk by my house

Hope you'll come around
You tell to come down
As I raise down my door
And ten minutes talk

But as the night came
And the stars and moon wave
I knew, I'm a fool
This love was never true
So I'm like forget you, forget you
Oh ooo

Leaning out the window
Saw your charming shadow
As you wave and smile say hello

Whisper to my friend
About this handsome man
And how he made me go mad
And how he made me go sad

But as the night came
And keep on waiting
I knew I'm a fool
This love was never true
So I'm like forget you, forget you
Oh ooo

Painting Lilian

Alone in the house
Singing this song
about you and I still miss you
But I have to forget you
Forget you
Ohhooo.hm

[Part II Faith]

Everything is going to be alright

With love comes faith, faith that everything will be all right. I had faith in friendships, my artwork was on track and I had gained quite some confidence. Exactly when I thought I had everything under control another chapter began - in the shape of a Big Apple.

New York, concrete jungle where dreams are made of (Alicia Keys)

My mom told me we were going to move to the USA to live in NYC. In New York! I had only seen New York City in television series like Gossip Girl. In my mind it was a magical place, a city where anything can happen. Being a Chinese girl, the idea of living in the western culture is something you only dream of. My mom used to tell me about classic English novels like Pride and Prejudice she had read when she was young. She had always seen that as a different, unreachable world. And now, it would in a way (as the US are not the UK but it is western, ah well, you know what I mean) be accessible to us. I could hardly believe it. It was November 2012 and I was in shock! My expectations were high, I would make new friends and do cool things; this was going to be such an adventure.

We went on a so called pre-visit at the end of February (2013) to find a school and an apartment and get a feel of what life was going to be like. I visited different schools where I was tested and interviewed. My mom and dad found an apartment close to Central Park. Oh my gosh, I couldn't believe it, Central Park! I felt like I stepped directly into the series Gossip Girl, which was true in a sense and I will get to that later.

Léman Manhattan School and Dwight School, both international private schools, were the schools I liked best. Dwight School had been around for more than a century and their International Baccalaureate (IB) program is acknowledged worldwide. IB basically prepares you for an education at highest-ranking Universities anywhere in the world. It would be more challenging than Léman school and my mom convinced me that I was ready for it, although I do remember our relocation agent saying: 'That is going to be tough'. It was an understatement that I only later grasped and totally ignored at the time. I simply was too excited.

Goodbye my darling Shanghai

We moved to New York City at the end of June 2013. The last month prior to the move was incredibly busy, everyone wanted to say goodbye and we had dinner parties all the time. I invited all my friends over for a farewell party at our house and sang them a song I wrote about Shanghai when I knew I was going to leave. People always talk about how dirty it is and that everyone spits on the streets, but to me it's so much more. It's the city where I made friends who taught me so much and - to me - is home. I wanted to make sure I would never forget that by capturing what is typical of Shanghai in a song. I sang 'My Darling Shanghai' to my friends at my farewell party as a gift to them and myself. It was a nice way to get over the process of saying goodbye and moving emotionally as well. Everyone started crying, even the boys. I found it very awkward, as I had never seen those guys cry that much before!

My Darling Shanghai
Scan the QR code on page 24 to listen the song

Tall buildings, cover with the smoky gray sky
Crazy driver is not following the sign
Strangers came up and ask your name
Just roll your eyes and walk away.
Weird people are blocking your way
The stupid traffic is making you late

#But I will never say
anything negative about you
I will never try to forget you

You will always be the stain in my heart
I hope you'll stay the same as always
I will miss you x4
Oh my darling Shanghai#

Kids are cutting the line
There are traffic noises all the time
Strangers come up and force you to buy their things
And there're people who spit everyday

Repeat #

You will always be the stain in my heart
I hope you'll stay the same as always
I will miss youx4

Oh my darling Shanghai
Waving at you saying goodbye
You wish me all the best and say
visit me if you have time.

Repeat #

Shanghai*

And then the moment was there. My dad and I were especially so freaking excited! We were full of adrenaline, kept on saying 'Once you can conquer NYC, you can conquer the world!' And we drove my mom crazy singing the chorus of Alicia Keys' The Empire State of Mind over and over again. Those lyrics will forever remind me of this period in my life: 'New York concrete jungle where dreams are made of, there's nothing you can't do.' It will be stuck in your head now but isn't it beautiful? When we saw the Statue of Liberty out of the window of the plane, we looked at each other: Now it was real.

The first weeks were awesome! My mom invited one of my best friends from Shanghai to help me settle in NYC, which turned the first weeks into a holiday. We explored the city together and ran around like tourists. We ate a burger at Shake Shack (oh my gosh, the BEST burger ever!) and when we walked up the stairs on Broadway, I felt completely happy and ready to rule this town! We immediately experienced that it's totally different than Hong Kong and Shanghai. It's so vibrant and inspiring and overwhelming.... and dirty! Oh my gosh, the subway is so gross, there's dog's poo on the streets and once I leaned against a wall I saw cockroaches, yuk! But I loved it anyway because hey, this is NYC, this is THE city and you don't complain about THE city. I loved the museums, art galleries and musical plays! People are busy, but they're busy doing fun and cultural things as well. And I was overwhelmed by all the nationalities living in this city. No one even asks you where you're from. It's totally different than Shanghai where nationalities other than Asian are always a minority.

While I loved this bubbly lifestyle, I had to get used to a few things as well. The fact that no-one made our beds, washed our clothes or ran our errands was definitely my number one complaint. I know! It embarrasses me now but I wasn't even aware that people actually do those things themselves. I didn't know any better as in Hong Kong and Shanghai we had someone taking care of our household tasks everyday. My mom was mostly shocked by the DIY situation. It doesn't only mean that you have to do everything yourself, but we suddenly realized that it also consumes so much time. My mom's least favorite chore was definitely grocery shopping daily. I can still hear her moaning carrying heavy bags in the kitchen: 'Can you imagine, we have to do all this even without a car?' Eating out is very expensive though and that's why we ate a lot of more affordable Central American food at street corners until my parents (and me, but only sometimes) finally started cooking themselves. My mom still calls NYC the DIY-city.

'I fell off my pink cloud with a thud' (Elizabeth Taylor)

When school started I had to get off my pink cloud and prepare for the next step of integrating. Luckily my new school had connected me with a girl who happened to live in the building next to ours. We had tea together with our moms and we immediately chitchatted as if we had been best friends forever. I'm totally not like that, which stipulated that it would be fine. I really looked forward to going to school. It would be easy as standards in Asia are high and my friends in Shanghai had assured me that I would do great.

When I walked through the 'School of Spirit Doors' at Dwight School in Manhattan though, I felt very special and privileged. The gateway to the school is comprised of double hand-forged iron doors that are beautiful and heavy. The doors are designed intentionally to be difficult to open. They symbolize that you have to make an effort to learn and that once inside Dwight's learning community you can feel safe. A parent who happens to be one of the leading metal smith artists in the world made the doors. Famous parents are Dwight parents, I learned later. I also learned later that the doors are never called the School of Spirit doors. They're called 'the very heavy, expensive doors'. Expensive because that's what teachers repeatedly tell us and heavy because they are twice my size and made of solid metal. It's especially annoying in wintertime when your hands are cold and you desperately want to enter the warm building.

But that was later! Now I walked through to the doors to enter a beautiful, almost 150 year old building with hundreds of screaming children and that's how my adventure at Dwight started.

New York*

People in NYC were super friendly but I wasn't sure if they meant it

I met new people, I instantly loved the teachers, but there was something weird about this school too. The students were super friendly, but I wasn't sure if they meant it. One of the first days a girl introduced herself to me. She asked me if I was new - she obviously wasn't - and we chitchatted a bit. When she spotted another girl from the corner of her eye she said: 'Oh my Gosh, that girl is so horrible, like don't ever talk to her'. A split second later they made eye contact, walked up to each other and hugged as if they were best friends. They hugged and teased me as well, even though I had never spoken with them before! Why would they do that? And what does a boy mean when you walk up together and another boy suddenly says: 'Hey dude, are you looking for some Chinese food?' That's just rude, right?

They would love my art-work until the most popular girl in school - the so-called Queen Bee - arrived, who didn't like me - and they would all ignore me and pretend they didn't like me either.

Even the few Asian kids in school were different. Most were younger and apart from the age-gap, these Chinese children grew up in the USA and were therefore called ABC's: American Born Chinese Children. I couldn't share my amazement and things that surprised or bothered me with them as they would never understand! Luckily I had my neighbor girlfriend, but I was used to having more friends than one. I started feeling left out and very lonely.

You have to peel off many layers to find the nice person underneath

The social circle I was confronted with at this school could have affected the social behavior that I found difficult to deal with. In Shanghai I went to an international school, but I could at least identify myself with the children who attended that school. Their parents were businessmen and businesswomen and we lived a similar life and lived in similar houses. I realize that we were very fortunate, but the people I met here at Dwight School were of another level of fortunate. Suddenly I attended the same school as children whose parents owned famous fashion shops such as Tiffany's, museums like the MOMA and were amongst the best metal smiths in the world.

I actually don't really care what parents do or how famous they are, I just wanted to make friends! It did intrigue me though because I noticed that having famous parents does something to these children. They are constantly protecting their background and work even harder than the others. If they don't get high grades, the spotlight will be on them and social media will be all over them. In a way, I could relate to them as I always feel that I have to represent the Chinese people. I have to get good grades to meet expectation of 'the people'. I too feel like I have to prove to them that some predictions people have are simply not true. They also encounter other people (children, teachers even) who want to be their friend because of their parents. There might be people that like them for who they are, but how would they know that for sure? They protect themselves with a lot of layers. An arrogant layer, an 'I'm unfriendly' layer and a 'don't touch me' layer. You have to peel off those layers in order to reach the nice person underneath the distant, arrogant, shallow person. I managed to do that, but in the beginning I had no clue. In the beginning I felt like a clueless Asian character in the series Gossip Girl.

Gossip Girl: We make our own fairytales

Because, Oh My Gosh, this school is the exact reflection of Gossip Girl. If you're not familiar with the series, it was broadcasted from 2007-2012 and was about students at an exclusive prep school on Manhattan's Upper East Side. I watched it in Shanghai and that's also why I couldn't believe my mom when she told me they had found an apartment in that same

Painting Lilian

Upper East Side of NYC. When I entered Dwight I could really relate; the drama, the arrogance, the parties in huge houses, the gossip and the fact that literally ALL the students are pretty, is exactly the same as my school. Normally you have a few smart children in a school that will definitely look and act like nerds. They have the glasses and the ugly sweater and they will make a joke at exactly the wrong moment. Not at Dwight though, basically everyone is pretty and smart and they study and they go out partying all night long as well. They are like Serena and Blake in the series; smart, pretty and to be admired in every way. They are not very friendly though, the peer pressure is ginormous and the curriculum extremely heavy. It's a tough combination.

Dwight School, New York*

My mom would call me lazy

I sometimes feel that I'm doing university work already and I'm not the only one. Last year I was studying for a biology exam with a friend and a man overheard us studying and walked up to us. He introduced himself, told us he was a biologist and asked which university we attended. We giggled and replied something like: 'No, no, we're just high-school students, we're only juniors!' Some of the subjects are indeed at university level. Which is good, because we can skip some of them, when we go to the university, but it doesn't make life easier right now. The Dwight program is on a very high theoretical level as well. It focuses especially on understanding art and the history of art. I had to write essays about paintings and painters and why they for example used a certain technique, color or perspective. Of course I grasp that I learn a lot from it, but creating art myself had always made me so happy!

I wasn't used to studying so hard. Sometimes I'm SO tired that I just have to sleep for an hour before I start doing my homework. I often work through the evening and I often only go to bed at midnight. A lot of students work really late hours. My mom didn't realize. Whenever she caught me sleeping she would get upset and call me lazy. She would try to explain that I was not the only one suffering from a lot of schoolwork. She would tell me about her prestigious secondary school. She just told me that she had to work very hard and manage to be in the top three of her school. If she achieved it her parents would have to pay less school-fees. She also said that she was confronted with children of really wealthy parents and that you just have to deal with it. You are the odd one out, so adjust; they're probably very nice. In other words, she had been there and it couldn't be that hard for me. I totally got it, but I don't think she realized that all these words made it only worse.

[Part III Hope]

Surprise yourself with what you're capable of!

This new school with its strange kids and very hard curriculum, being away from my friends and not finding enough time to spend on my art and music just got to me. While I was studying, my friends from Shanghai posted their amazing art projects on Facebook. They were progressing and I felt like I was standing still. It was the worst feeling. I was so tired, I felt I was missing out socially and lost the ability to look at things with humor. I don't even remember one happy day of that period.

After two months in my new school - it must have been October 2013 - I had a nervous breakdown. I just couldn't deal with the situation anymore and cried myself to sleep every single night. But crying myself to sleep was not the worst thing, I needed control and I found a way.

Eat your heart out

I have never been a skinny girl, but I had never been obsessed with my weight either. My dad of course is a salsa dancer and busy all day. My mom exercises but only when she gains weight. My mom has been obsessed with my weight, but only when I was younger. I was a pretty big baby and she told me that I had become quite big when I had lived with my grandparents for a while prior to our move to Shanghai. Upon prompting from my dad I started cross-country and stuck to my Paleo diet again. That's how I lost my puppy fat. I immediately stopped with cross-country when I reached my normal weight as I'm not a huge fan of exercising. How much I weigh is not a top priority, I believe it's a waste of time and energy to be obsessed with weight. And I love food!

I do belong to the group of people that start eating more when they are stressed though. So when I didn't feel happy in NYC I started eating more. There really wasn't one trigger point. The most important factors were that I didn't have any really close friends, the IB program was very hard, I couldn't release stress by practicing arts and I missed my friends in Shanghai like crazy. Whenever I felt unhappy, I snacked. And I felt unhappy ALL the time. I especially craved sweet things, which I'm not supposed to eat because of Tourette's. But I craved sweet things, that my mom and dad never noticed still surprises me. One day, I don't even remember when exactly, I ate way too much again. I felt so bad and desperately wanted to get rid of that feeling. That's when I vomited for the first time.

It just happened. And it was so easy that it just happened again and again.

What is bulimia precisely?

One day I just ate way too much and felt horrible. Of course I knew about bulimia and I knew I could stick a finger in my throat, but I never realized it was fairly easy to do. It was. It actually was surprisingly easy and that's why it happened again and again. I guess eating a lot (I later learned that it's called 'binging') and purging became my safe place, although I felt horrible about it at the same time. I think for me the hardest part was living with this secret, keeping it away from my mom and my best friends. It felt like I betrayed them and I felt ashamed.

In official words you could describe Bulimia Nervosa as follows:

A person with Bulimia Nervosa binges on food regularly and feels a loss of control. Binging involves eating large amounts of high-calorie foods over a short period. When the binge starts it is extremely difficult to stop. Some patients say they consume the food so fast that they hardly taste it. The binge is followed by a feeling of guilt and shame, which leads to compensatory actions, such as self-induced vomiting, over-exercising, not eating, and overusing diuretics, enemas or laxatives. A lot of girls suffer from Bulimia. The National Health Service in the UK, states that up to 8% of females probably have had or will have Bulimia Nervosa at some time in their lives. That there are a lot of us doesn't mean we can't help it. You have to search for help!

I didn't exercise excessively and didn't use any medications. I did feel ashamed and I didn't stop eating either. I guess I had 'bulimia light' and maybe that was the reason that I could think clearly and search for help after a few months. Eventually telling my mom helped make it real. When you tell it to someone who is close to you and whom you love, there's no way back. You're not doing it for yourself, you're doing it for your loved ones.

I don't think my mom or friends could have been able to help me. What I've learned from this process is that only I can make myself happy. What really helped me was taking the first step. When I let go of self-pity and took control over my life by making decisions, positive things started to happen. It's how life works, it can be amazing, but you have to work for it.

Self portrait in my Manhattan home, 2014

I didn't talk to anyone about my problems. I didn't feel safe enough which was part of the problem. I only shared some of it with my mom. Not the bulimia part though, as I thought she would never understand. I told her I missed Shanghai and my friends and that I desperately wished to go home over Christmas. I tried to explain that I really needed peace and friendly faces, because integrating was harder than I thought. Instead of listening to my problems, mom gave motivational speeches like: 'You will be good, you will be fine.' and 'Do your best.' She also asked me to please stop whining with a desperate voice. It didn't really help. Her pep talks were quite superficial, but I guess she was just clocked up in her work and settling in. I didn't really care anyway, I just wanted to go to Shanghai and when I started screaming it in the hope she would finally listen she would calmly reply: 'Well, that's not possible, we decided to move and we will be here for at least three years,

Lilian.' You know it's the end of the discussion when your parents say your name out loud, so annoying.

They just didn't understand me

My parents stressed that it was too expensive for a trip back home during the holiday season and they wouldn't want me to go on my own. They kept comparing my situation to theirs when they were young, again. It made me the big complainer, from their point of view. Of course they had a point; my mom would tell me again that she grew up in a house with four families and worked hard to get where she is right now. My dad never lets an occasion pass to tell me that his family was the only Chinese speaking family in Bolivia and look where it got him! I am aware of it and appreciate it.

On the other hand though, they did have a lot of opportunities back in the days (as they would say). When my parents were young the world was changing rapidly and the economy was waiting for youngsters that had attended good schools. They never had to worry about getting a job as they would get a wonderful job in a heartbeat. Nowadays, the economy is slow, my generation will have to work hard to find their place in this world. I'm aware of it every single day as bright, pretty Dwight-children surround me. They all speak several languages and they all have the most successful parents who will provide them with all these opportunities. It's a rat race; how can you standout when everyone else is brilliant? Yes, I'm privileged being able to attend this school, I'm privileged that we're living in this house and I'm privileged having all these choices. Choices my parents didn't have or at least worked very hard for. I understood it all, but it would have been great if they had listened to me carefully for a change.

Looking back now, I think our expectations were too high. We were so happy in Shanghai and so excited about moving to New York, the city where dreams are supposed to come true. We thought we would 'just do it'. When dreams didn't come true fast enough, all three of us couldn't deal with it happily. The move was a downfall for the family at that moment. We all missed Shanghai like crazy, but I also realized we had to take control again. We had to get it together and be happy again and I realized we had to stop blaming the move.

Fighting my way up

Somehow I managed to look at my dreadful situation with a helicopter view. Maybe I could because I felt I had no choice. It was either steeling myself or drowning in my misery. One day I just walked up to my parents, firmly stood in front of them and blurted out:

'I want to leave Dwight School. I'm done with the pressure, the drama and the lack of an art program that I really like.'

I wanted to add more arguments such as that I really needed a less stressful environment without heavy iron doors and that I would do anything for a switch. I was prepared for a battle! But they just said yes. I could see that they weren't wholeheartedly supportive, but they said I could switch if I really wanted to.

Wait, what?! I could switch, just like that?

All of a sudden I had a choice again. I had to let this sink in for a while as choosing is loosing and the power to decide made me doubtful. Wouldn't switching schools make me feel as if I was running away, as if I was escaping my fears? That was not what I had envisioned to happen in New York! I would finish high school and I chose this school for a reason! I suddenly felt that if I could finish Dwight, I could conquer the world. Wasn't that what my dad and I had been singing over and over when we had just arrived to New York? Suddenly I felt so strong, this was my dream, my concrete jungle! In a split second I changed my mind 180 degrees and decided to stay at Dwight.

A few weeks later we ran into a friend of my mom's whose daughter attended Parsons, a very well known fashion design school. A lot of famous people attended this school. It's hugely expensive, but the best of the best as well. The daughter was super-enthusiastic about it and I felt butterflies in my stomach. My mom and I looked at each other. This could definitely be the solution to my art struggle! I had been trying to practice art myself for a while, but I figured that I needed assignments and I needed someone to guide me in the process. My mom and dad were willing to let me attend Parsons for one semester. I got to follow one of their pre-college programs held every Saturday morning! I was SO excited, this really gave me back my life!

It felt like making decisions created room for a positive flow. I really was on the way up and at the same time I knew I had one more challenge to face. It was the biggest problem and for this one, I realized, I needed help.

I had to unveil my deepest secret. I had been keeping my eating disorder a secret for so long that unveiling it felt like betraying myself. That sounds strange right? But I have no clue how to describe it otherwise. My parents didn't even know I had a disease, let alone that I would see the school counselor. I didn't want them to worry, especially now that they were doing their best to help me. They would feel guilty and take it personal and that would make me feel even more horrible. I really needed someone who knew nothing about me and with whom I could talk without being judged.

So I was really going to see the school counselor, oh my gosh! I couldn't care less if anyone, classmates or teachers would see me, because I just wanted to get rid of my problem. I had reached the point that I couldn't care about what people thought of me. The counselor greeted me with a soft voice. I felt like a patient, but at the same time I did not because consulting him was my own choice.

He was really nice and friendly and as soon as I started talking, I got so emotional. I cried and cried and couldn't stop, I literally finished his whole tissue box. I have no clue what happened, I'm almost never emotional, it came from a place deep down. I told him about the stress, the bulimia and that my parents didn't understand me. I shared that they kept comparing their situations and youth to mine, which made me so angry. That they were so nice these past weeks and that it had made me feel so guilty! He listened, he gave me a shoulder to cry on and by doing that soothed my guilt, my anger and my fears. Nothing more, nothing less, but it was exactly what I needed.

Only I could make myself happy again

The counselor connected me to a social worker in the hospital. I remember going there a few days later on my own again. It was very cold and I was walking really fast to stay warm. I remember how I suddenly slowed down, looked up and felt the need to inform my mom. I think I was excited in a way to be doing this on my own and definitely being on my way back to normal. Instead of a heavy heart I felt so alive for the first time in a long time. I sent her a text message because she was out of town. She was so relieved that I had told her. She must have known something as I can still hear the excited tone in her reply. I promised to tell her everything when she got back to New York that same evening.

While I was waiting for the counselor I looked around and saw a lot of sad faces. These boys and girls looked like they were going to die. I wondered if I had had that expression just months, maybe weeks before? It scared me, what had happened to me? I knew I looked so much better now than they did, I didn't feel like I belonged there. I had taken action and was on my way back. I did stay though and spoke with the social worker. It was a very nice woman and I again shared my story with a total stranger. She told me the only one that could make a change was me. Only I could make myself happy. It's something that I knew, but sometimes it's so much easier to blame it on something. It makes you feel like it's not in your circle of influence. The things she said were very true. She also advised me to surround myself with people I truly like to hang out with; people that are friendly and can make me happy.

Of course I knew that already, but to hear it from someone else gives new meaning to already existing words. While on my way to schedule a new appointment I decided I wouldn't go back. The hassle and the waste of time I foresaw made me walk passed the administration desk. I decided that I should and could do it myself from there.

I sang her all the songs I had ever written

Even though I couldn't focus on my art projects, I always kept writing songs, when I felt down and horrible. I'm mostly inspired when I'm not happy. A very good friend from Shanghai asked me to write her a song, but I could only do it when we were miles apart and I dearly missed her (that's the song: 'Hey Maddy'). It was the only way I could truly express my feelings. My mom didn't even know that I could sing and that I could play the guitar so well. When my mom came back to NYC I decided to open up completely. She walked into my room and I said something like: 'Well sit down mom, I'd like to sing to you.' I quickly grabbed my guitar, I wouldn't give myself time to change my mind. I sang her all the songs I had ever written, starting with 'Bird' and then on to the ones I wrote in the darker period in my life. It was a surprise to her and her expression was beautiful.

> ***Hey Maddy***
> ***Scan the QR code on page 24 to listen the song***
>
> *Hey Maddy how you've been its really been a while*
> *I always wanna write you a song*
> *But end up skipping and you waited so long*

Hey Maddy here I am singing this song for you..
It's kinda crappy but I know you will
Love it anyway.

#Da da la da da dala da
Everything will stay the same
Da da da da da da da
Nothing will ever change#

Hey Maddy please tell me the truth did you miss me, cuz I miss you
It's been a year since I played for you
Now you can listen to the song anytime after school

Repeat #

Oh Maddy you're so sweet, you're the sunshine on my cheek.
Oh Maddy you're more than a friend, you are my best friend
Oh Maddy will it be the same, in 10 years time?

Oh my my my my Maddy
Oh my my my my Maddy

Hey Maddy remember those days we both got our heart breaks.
We screamed we shouted and we let it out. We run around like clowns.

Hey Maddy are you too old now to do those things
But I really really miss those days and don't want it to change.

I also shared with her that I had bulimia and she suddenly understood why I had not been feeling well, didn't sleep well and why my bathroom and especially toilet had been so dirty. Oh my gosh, she had noticed it! I felt ashamed, but by the looks of it I think my mom felt worse. She told me that she had seen my text on her way to an important meeting. It made her feel like a horrible mom as she had been so busy with settling in herself that she had no clue that I was feeling this bad. She told me that it has been very difficult for her finding her way in a totally different culture too. I think I was most relieved when she told me that it was unfair of her to compare her situation to mine, which had maybe put too much pressure on me.

I wanted to inspire young girls with my music

I know my mom spoke with my Dean. That's okay, I guess she needed someone to share her feelings with as well. And she also immediately figured out ways to help me. Of course she did, it's deeply rooted in her to turn negative emotions into positive action. We had faced and dealt with difficulties before and she had helped me when we discovered I had Tourette's. My mom probably thought she paced herself, but she didn't wait too long to share her idea to create a mini concert of my songs. The concert would be a good way of raising money in order to help others. She had recently visited Africa and wanted to raise money for an organization that helps schools in need with computers for example. We brainstormed a plan and thought of producing an album. Helping others was what I was aiming for, but it also gave me a real goal, which made me focus and create better than ever.

Of course we had no experience, but when my mom has something in mind, she will make it happen. She lives by the idea that you don't have to be a professional on day one. Just take it step by step and see how far we can get by having a little faith in our imagination and creativity. Let's surprise ourselves with what we're capable of!

My school in Shanghai connected me with the quickly expanding International Women's Academy (IWA), based in Shanghai. We instantly felt this was the right connection. The IWA is always in search of ways to empower women to become future leaders. I became their NYC ambassador and we organized three charity concerts starting in June 2014; one in Shanghai, one in Manhattan (NYC) and one in Buffalo City (New York). I played my guitar, sang my songs and we sold my first charity album "Follow Me" and some merchandise such as t-shirts and cotton recycled bags with my artwork printed on them. The money we raised benefited Ndoombo Orphanage linked to the International Women's Academy and located in Duluti Arusha in Tanzania. With the donated money they could purchase computers for their school. It made my heart happy to be able to contribute to a good cause, while doing something that I love.

A collection of my artworks

"Follow Me" charity concert in NYC, Dec 2014

Performed in "Hope & a Future" event and Barnes
& Noble bookstore in Buffalo City 2015

Something else that also definitely helped me to gain back some self-confidence funnily enough had something to do with school. There are different opportunities to be active besides normal school work and there's one network activity that I like a lot. I joined the Global Issues Network, GIN in March 2014. The group consists of the more nerdy kids in school and I actually like hanging out with them. The group comes together every Wednesday and we discuss global issues and figure out which subject we could use for the yearly international meeting. These international meetings are the best! You get to talk about global issues with networks representing other schools from all over the world.

After a selection process of several months, I was chosen to represent Dwight School on a tour to Luxembourg together with seven other students. It was fascinating! We got to meet Maria Theresa, the grand Duchesse of Luxembourg and prepared a presentation about gender equality, which was the main subject of the Luxembourg trip. A lot of governments were represented through their embassy people. I realized it's a great platform for teenagers, you finally feel that you're heard by decision makers.

The Global Issue Network Conference in Luxembourg, April 2014

When we kissed, violins played

When you bring 300 teenagers together, of course there is a lot of chemistry and a lot of fun between boys and girls. I enjoy the mix of serious work and acting a bit silly though. So I partied a bit with my team and the funny thing is I met this very interesting guy. We discovered we had a lot in common; we could chat forever. He was a serious swimmer and I love people that have a passion and focus on something they're good at. I could act silly with him and we had so much fun. We also discovered that he had lived in Shanghai, where he went to an International school together with some of my friends. Isn't it weird that we had never met before? He was very easy to read, a genuine, friendly guy and cute too. I liked that he was really tall, well over 6 feet and way taller than me.

The week went amazingly fast and all of a sudden it was our last evening! There was a big dinner we went to with the whole group. When we all walked back to the hotel, this guy and I secretly took a different route. Suddenly we stopped on the steps of a beautiful building. I knew what we were about to do, oh my gosh! When he kissed me it started drizzling and music started to play. I heard violins and piano tunes and it was all so unrealistic and amazing! When we looked up I saw something that must have been a church. I felt like we were playing a movie scene. Later I looked the place up and it was the Grand Ducal Palace, which is really old and has a lot of history. Isn't it romantic? I felt so good, it was like it was meant to be!

Unfortunately it didn't last, as long distance relationships at this age just don't work. There is too much to discover in the world to commit yourself to someone this early in life. I felt sad, but the positive outtake is that it gave me faith that there are some really nice boys on this planet that can turn my world upside down. I even wrote a song about it: 'Until May'. When I told my mom she said something like 'Date who-ever you want now, but please, come to your senses when you're older, marry a decent guy!' As if I would date a weird guy? These events in my life especially made me realize that I like boys that are genuine, that I can trust and are cute at the same time. It's a tough combination to find, I'm totally aware of that, but I won't settle for less because I'm worth it. Wow, that I can say that just like that took me a long time.

Palace of the grand dukes Luxembourg *

Conclusion

February 2016 - Living in the here and now

I've taken you on a journey through my life, my family history and my ups and downs. Sharing a rough period of my life with you wasn't easy, but I'm glad I did. It was insightful for me to reflect on what has happened. Besides that, what happened to me could happen to you too. I've learned that life comes with ups and downs and that it's okay! Just embrace everything and keep communicating with people that are close to you. Don't exclude them and don't be ashamed, they probably have experienced something similar in their lives. Share your problems with 'your special someone'; your best friend, your teacher, or like me, your mom. Sharing my problems with my mom helped me owning the problem and climbing out of the dark hole I had fallen into.

We've been in NYC for close to three years and I've almost finished my senior year at The Dwight School. It's still a tough curriculum, but I'm very proud that I've made the decision to finish it. Since the beginning of the school year I've worked on applications for various Universities around the globe. I've really come to love NYC and I would like to stay here and continue my education here in future. On the other hand, now that I've conquered NYC, I truly feel that I can make it anywhere! Painting is my passion and I love making music. From that perspective a school like

Parsons would be great, but life can be unexpected. I will have to wait patiently where I will be accepted and choose wisely. It might be New York, but I might choose to study in another country and take on a new challenge! I believe that every decision will open a door to a new chapter in my life, with opportunities of becoming a better and stronger person.

The last few months have been amazing with regards to my creative career. I have developed an interest for 'Bachata', a Latino genre of music my dad often dances to. Chinese Bachata dancers wholeheartedly dance to these Latin beats and I wanted to give them a song they could understand as well. That's why I've written and produced two Chinese Bachata songs: *I will always love you* 一直愛著你 and: *I don't want to think about you* 不再想起你. Other fabulous news is that I'm accepted to exhibit during the ArtExpo New York 2016, which takes place in April.

Download the "QR code" app, and scan this code to listen the song

What else? I've made beautiful friends, had a few flings, but nothing serious and I turned 18 in December! Oh my gosh, 18, I'm so old now! My mom, dad and I celebrated it together. I loved that, it was great to be together as a family and reflect on life and our NYC adventure in particular.

We've all had a rough time in the beginning and we've all fallen in love with this city in the end. This city that never sleeps, is filled with opportunities, where it's either too hot, or too cold and is extremely expensive. We love the vibes and moreover, we settled in; we made friends, discovered favorite places to eat, drink and hang out. We became part of the city and yes, I believe you could state that we are New Yorkers now!

I've enjoyed sharing my story with you, my first loves, my hopes and dreams. I feel like I've grown from Lilian to Liane on so many levels. I'm very curious what life has in store for me. I feel strong and ready, bring it on!

Love Liane

<u>超越自己 Be a Better Me</u>
Scan the QR code on page 24 to listen the song

來到一個陌生世界 *Entering a strange world,*
一種冰冷的感覺 *It is cold.*
抬起頭 *Raise your head,*
繼續走 *Keep moving on,*
你的未來在前頭 *Your future is there for you.*

張開眼睛 *Open your eyes,* 充分利用 *Make the most,*
寶貴生命 *Of your precious life.*
放開自己 *Let it go.*

如果你哭 *If you cry,*
你就哭到底 *Just cry.*
明天超越自己 *Tomorrow, I will be a better me.*

#我不會停 *I will not stop,*
我要飛到那顆星星 *I will reach for the stars.*
我不會停 *I will not stop,*

我會跳進懸崖的谷底 I will fall into the bottom of the valley.
我會前進 I will move forward,
嘗試著拿第一 Try to be the champion.
我不回頭 I will not look back,
我會朝著那光明 I will face (the) brightness.
我會超越自己 And be a Better Me.
超越自己 Be a Better Me.
Be a Better me.
Be a Better me.#

站在一個 Standing in,
殘酷境界 A cruel reality,
一種刺疼的感覺 It's a feeling of pain.
挺起胸 Stand tall,
向前沖 Run forward,
你會跳越成功的盡頭 You will leap forward and reach success.
摸干眼淚 Wipe your tears,
不要心碎 No heartbreak,
你的汗血沒有白費 Your sweat and effort is not wasted.
站在這裡 Standing here,
也是為了證明 Just to prove,
得到大家的尊敬 And to earn the respect.
Repeat #

聽到掌聲 The sound of applause,
我也就安心 Calms my soul,
沒有白費我的努力 As my effort is not wasted.

*我不會停 I will not stop,
我要飛到那顆星星 I will reach for the stars.
我不會停 I will not stop,
我會跳進懸崖的谷底 I will fall into the bottom of the valley.
我會前進 I will move forward,

嘗試著拿第一 *Try to be the champion.*
我不回頭 *I will not look back*
我會朝著那光明 *I will face the brightness.*
我會超越自己 *And be a Better Me.*
超越自己 *Be a Better Me.*
Be a Better me.
Be a Better me.

Young artists at Dwight School, New York.

The Global Issue Network in Milan, 2015

ArtExpo, New York 2016, at Pier 94 – one of the
world's biggest art shows. www.LianeChu.com

Dear daughter

Dear Lilian,

I remember holding you in my arms when you were just born, our little bundle of joy. I remember singing you Chinese songs my mom used to sing to me and I remember the fun we had with the three of us. We share a love for food and I see a combination of your father's creativity and rays of light and my dedication and ability to focus reflected in you. I witnessed how you became a girl, a teenager, how you made friends for life and grew into this sweet, creative and independent girl.

Maybe I figured you were more independent then you really were when we moved to New York. You were only 15, still a child! Maybe I pushed you too hard discussing possible schools and I thought IB would be good for you. I certainly underestimated the social challenges that come with an international move. When you shut down and had a hard time being happy and bubbly, I felt something wasn't right. When you had a hard time waking up in the morning, I sensed you were suffering. When I dropped you at school and saw you walk through the doors, your shoulders hanging, it broke my heart. But I didn't know what to do. I hoped things would get better, that time would heal.

I too had to adjust to our new life and the process of integrating at work took me way longer than I had expected. Work required all my social strengths and home turned into a 'household operation', also due to the DIY nature of this city. It's no excuse, I should have taken time off to be with you and reflect on what was really important. My motivational speeches weren't enough and I definitely shouldn't have compared your situation to mine when I was young. You are so right; every generation faces their own problems. I was so focused on keeping my head above sea level and swimming as fast as I could, that I didn't realize you were drowning right behind me. I'm so thankful that you screamed for help.

I remember it clearly. It was February 11th, 2014, very cold and I was on my way to a very important meeting when my phone beeped. You texted me:

> *Mom, I don't want you to worry, I will be all right, but I want you to know that I'm on my way to the hospital. I've been having an eating disorder for a while and searched for help. I will tell you everything when you're back home. Please don't worry, it will be alright!*

Someone had thrown you a lifebuoy and I felt extremely bad and relieved at the same time. Bad because it should have been me who had come to the rescue. Relieved because I could pursue my meeting knowing things would get better.

Things did get better. The day you grabbed your guitar and sang me all the songs you had ever written was one of the best days of my life. You were so strong and vulnerable at the same time.

I could see how sad you had been, I could see what you had gone through and I could see how strong you had become. Happiness surrounded you again and you created it yourself. I wish I had been there for you more, to guide you, but I wasn't, and I'm so sorry about that. I guess parenting is a continuously learning on the job experience and I definitely grew during this period in our lives. I think all three of us have learned and grown a lot.

Your story of love, faith and hope has taught me valuable life lessons.

You taught me that showing your weaknesses can be your strength.

You taught me that you can only make yourself happy and that you have a choice to do so.

You taught me that only love counts and that you have to put an effort in loving.

Lilian, my bao bei, I'm so incredibly proud of you and I love you.

Mom

About the Author

Eva Lebens is an independent writer and accomplished illustrator from the Netherlands. She has written blogs, columns, and articles. Interviews are her particular favorite. She illustrates her own writing in addition to works for other authors.

Lebens lived in South Africa and the United States for five years, which provided the opportunity to achieve fluency in English. She currently lives with her husband Joost and their three amazing children in The Hague, Netherlands.

Soto Ayam - Indonesian version of chicken soup, is a clear herbal broth, served with a boiled

egg, fried shallots, celery leaves, rice noodles and herbs.

Gloria Food - Shop 6, G/F, Wang Yip Building, 2-26 Ka Lok Street, Kwun tong, Hong Kong

With my friends in Shanghai (YCIS)

Painting Lilian

My sweet 16th birthday in Manhattan, 2014

Painting is what I love, Manhattan 2015

My Asian friends in New York.Won

Silver Awards with my Best Friend, Yun Fei Liu International Youth Talent Competition, Houston July 2015

"SQUAD"-An American slang indicating a group of friends

* Remarks : Photos taken from Internet, Google Website.
Website : www.lianechu.com

Acknowledgement

I'd like to thank a few dear friends who found time within their busy schedule to give me their honest feedback. Their valuable advice helped Eva and me in completing this book. Thanks to Sarah Breimer, Machteld Henzel and Melissa Groom for professionally editing the book. They're very talented and are close connections of Eva Lebens, the author.

Thank you to Hailun Zhou who helped following through all the tedious operating processes that come with publishing a book and in making this book available online. I'd like to thank Simon Bell, Bakani Ntaisi, Emma Dean & Rebeca Cardona who provided their feedback on our first draft. It helped us to improve and resulted in this latest version. A special thank you goes to all those who took time and effort to write commentaries; I loved reading them. These unique short messages provided thoughtful feedback and recognition for this book.

Lilian and I treasure the hours of conversation we had with Eva Lebens. She is someone you immediately trust and want to share your life story with. Her inspiration, patience and dedication to create an easy to read book for all nationalities out of all the information she gathered is amazing.

Finally, my deepest gratitude goes to Holly Breach who provided her instant support and practical advice dealing with a teenage girl. Her experience and wisdom being a mother to three successful and talented children was a huge help to me.

Thank you all for your Love, Faith and Hope both for me and for this book.

Maggie Chan

Made in the USA
Middletown, DE
13 June 2022